Nature's Cycles

The Plant Cycle

Sally Morgan

PowerKiDS
press™

New York

Published in 2009 by The Rosen Publishing Group Inc.
29 East 21st Street, New York, NY 10010

First Edition

Series editor: Nicola Edwards
Designer: Jason Billin

Library of Congress Cataloging-in-Publication Data

Morgan, Sally.
   The plant cycle / Sally Morgan. — 1st ed.
       p. cm. — (Nature's cycles)
   Includes index.
   ISBN 978-1-4358-2867-4 (library binding)
   ISBN 978-1-4358-2949-7 (paperback)
   ISBN 978-1-4358-2953-4 (6-pack)
   1. Plants—Juvenile literature. 2. Plant life cycles—Juvenile literature.
   I. Title.
   QK49.M8567 2009
   580—dc22

                              2008025771

Manufactured in China

Picture acknowledgments: Cover: Main image Paul Thompson/Ecoscene;
flower Robert Pickett Ecoscene – Papilio; germinating seed Sally Morgan/
Ecoscene; beans in pod Seaspring Photos/ Ecoscene

Title page: Paul Thompson/ Ecoscene; p2 Stuart Baines/ Ecoscene; p3 Robert
Pickett Ecoscene – Papilio; p4 Sally Morgan/ Ecoscene; p5 Robert Pickett
Ecoscene – Papilio; p7 (t, b) Frank Blackburn/ Ecoscene; p8 Chinch
Gryniewicz/ Ecoscene; p9 (t) Sally Morgan/ Ecoscene, (b) Alan Towse/
Ecoscene; p10 Fritz Polking/ Ecoscene; p11 Robert Pickett Ecoscene –
Papilio; p12 Seaspring Photos/ Ecoscene; p13 (t) Sally Morgan/ Ecoscene, (b)
Rod Smith/ Ecoscene; p14 Wayne Lawler/ Ecoscene; p15 Sally Morgan/
Ecoscene; p16 Vicki Coombs/ Ecoscene; p17 Robert Pickett Ecoscene –
Papilio; p18 Robert Pickett Ecoscene – Papilio; p19 William Dunn /
Ecoscene – Papilio; p21 (tl) Anthony Cooper/ Ecoscene, (tr) Guy
Menendez/ Ecoscene, (b) Andrew Brown/ Ecoscene; p22 Fritz
Polking/ Ecoscene; p23 (t) Robert Pickett Ecoscene – Papilio,
(b) Sally Morgan/ Ecoscene; p24 Kjell Sandved/ Ecoscene; p25
Sally Morgan/ Ecoscene; p26 (t, ml, b) Sally Morgan/ Ecoscene,
(mr) Chinch Gryniewicz/ Ecoscene; p27 Rob Nichol/ Ecoscene;
p28 Stuart Baines/ Ecoscene; p29 (t) Wayne Lawler/ Ecoscene,
(b) Edward Bent/ Ecoscene

Artwork by Ian Thompson

Contents

What is a plant?   4

Leaves, stems, and roots   6

Photosynthesis   8

Plants and their environment   10

Seeds   12

New life   14

Flowers   16

Plant reproduction   18

Fruits and seeds   20

Spreading seeds   22

Runners, stolons, and bulbs   24

Rotting plants   26

Plants and global warming   28

Glossary   30

Further Information and Web Sites   31

Index   32

What is a plant?

Plants grow all around us. They provide us with food and shelter. Without plants, humans and other animals could not survive. There are hundreds of thousands of different types of plant. They range in size from tiny algae that are found floating in water, to huge trees such as redwoods and eucalyptuses.

Making food

Plants differ from animals, because they can make their own food. They can do this because they have a green pigment in their leaves and stems that captures light energy from the sun. Plants use this energy to combine carbon dioxide and water to make sugars and starches. This food-making process is called photosynthesis. The food is used for growth to produce new mass. The living mass of a plant is called biomass.

In Focus: Animals need plants

Plants are called producers because they can make their own food. Animals cannot make their own food, so they rely on plants for food, either directly or indirectly. Herbivores are animals that obtain all the food they require by eating plants. Carnivores are animals that eat other animals for food. Although carnivores do not eat plants, they feed on plant-eating animals. An omnivore is an animal that eats a mix of plant and animal foods.

⬖ The giant sequoia is the world's largest tree, growing to a height of more than 262 feet (80 meters), with a trunk that weighs several tons.

In Focus: Plant groups

Scientists place plants into different groups according to their features. The most familiar group is made up of flowering plants. Another group is formed by cone-bearing plants, for example, trees such as pine and spruce. The seeds develop inside the cones. Ferns are a group of plants that do not produce any flowers or cones. Their leaves are called fronds and they lack proper roots. They grow in damp, shady places. Growing in these damp places, too, are mosses and liverworts, small plants that are also without proper roots.

▶ Animals such as this giant panda are plant eaters or herbivores. The giant panda is dependent on the bamboo plant for 99 percent of its diet.

The plant cycle

The largest group of plants is the flowering plants, the plants that produce flowers. Common flowering plants include roses, daisies, dandelions, and trees such as oak and beech. In this book, you will learn about the life cycle of flowering plants. Each life cycle starts with a seed that germinates and grows into a new plant. The plant grows larger, producing new leaves, and later, flowers. Then seeds are produced, allowing the cycle to start all over again.

Leaves, stems, and roots

A plant is made up of a shoot and a root. The shoot is the part of a plant that is above ground, and it consists of leaves and stems. A plant's roots anchor it in the ground. Most plants grow gradually larger through their life.

Plant cells

Look closely at part of a plant under a microscope and you will see that it is made up of tiny building blocks called cells. Each plant cell is surrounded by a wall made of a tough material called cellulose, which gives the cell shape and support.

Beneath the wall is a thin membrane, a little like a skin, which encloses a jellylike substance called cytoplasm. Floating in the cytoplasm is the nucleus, the control center of the cell, and a fluid-filled space called a vacuole.

Cells that can photosynthesize contain round structures called chloroplasts. Each chloroplast is packed with a green pigment called chlorophyll, which plays an important role in photosynthesis.

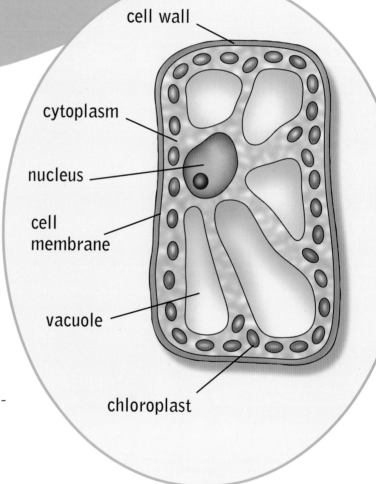

cell wall

cytoplasm

nucleus

cell membrane

vacuole

chloroplast

⬥ This is how a typical plant cell would look when viewed under a microscope.

6

Investigate: Deciduous and evergreen leaves

Deciduous plants drop their leaves once a year and replace them with new ones, but evergreen plants drop a few leaves all the time. This leaf fall helps plants to survive cold weather and drought.
Compare the leaves of plants in a park or yard, e.g. needle-shaped pine leaves and broader-shaped oak leaves, and decide whether they are evergreen or deciduous.

⬤ Some leaves have a simple oval shape, but others are made up of several leaflets joined together.

Shoots and roots

The parts of a plant that grow above the ground are involved with photosynthesis, transport, and reproduction. The stem holds the leaves and flowers in position. Inside the stem are specialized cells that form tubes to carry water, nutrients, and food around the plant.

Large plants such as trees make wood, a tough material that gives them extra support. Plants take in water and minerals from the ground through their roots. The most important part of the root system is the root hair. This has threadlike extensions that grow out into the soil and take in water.

In Focus: Plant parasites

The dodder is a weird plant. It looks more like a piece of colored plastic than a plant. It is not green, because it does not make its own food. Instead, it is orange or yellow. Dodders are parasites, because they get their food from other plants. They twine themselves around another plant and send out tiny growths into the plant's stems to suck out food. This harms the plant because it does not get enough food for its growth.

◀ The orange twine is really the stem of a dodder plant. It is growing over and feeding off of a heather plant.

Photosynthesis

Plants are self-feeding organisms, able to make their own food from the sunlight, air, and water around them. Animals do not have this ability, and so are reliant on "ready-made" food in the form of plants or other animals.

Making food

A plant makes most of its food in its leaves. A typical leaf consists of a flat blade, crisscrossed by a network of veins. Most leaves are broad and thin, which allows them to capture as much light as possible. Some leaves have a short stem called a petiole that joins the leaf to the stem. The petiole moves the leaf into the best position to receive light.

Inside the leaf, the light is trapped by chlorophyll in the chloroplasts.

Sunlight is not the only requirement for photosynthesis. The plant also needs carbon dioxide, a gas that is found in air. Carbon dioxide enters a leaf through tiny pores called stomata. Another necessary raw material is water. This is absorbed by the roots and carried up through the stem and then along veins in the leaf.

During the day, the plant uses light energy to join carbon dioxide and water to make sugar and oxygen. Some of the oxygen moves out of the leaves through the stomata and the rest is used by the plant.

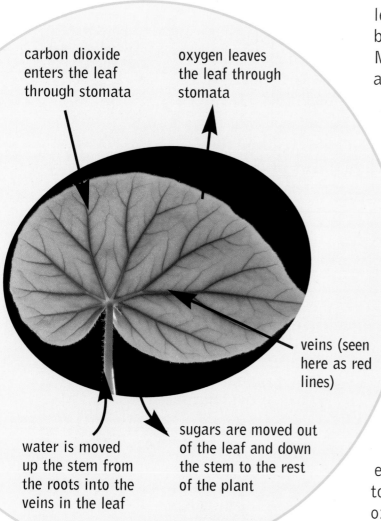

carbon dioxide enters the leaf through stomata

oxygen leaves the leaf through stomata

veins (seen here as red lines)

water is moved up the stem from the roots into the veins in the leaf

sugars are moved out of the leaf and down the stem to the rest of the plant

Investigate: Oxygen from pondweed

It is difficult to see a plant photosynthesizing, because the gases involved are invisible. However, it is possible to see oxygen bubbling from the leaves of a pondweed in water. Take a piece of pondweed and place it in a jar of pond water. Place the jar in a bright place, such as under a table lamp or on a sunny window ledge. Soon you will see tiny bubbles of oxygen rising from the plant.

Moving food around

The sugar can be used by the plant in different ways. Some is carried through the stem to other parts of the plant, especially the tips of the shoot and root where growth is taking place. The sugar may be made into other essential substances such as fat and protein, which the plant needs for growth. Any sugar that is left over is transported to the roots, where it is stored as starch for future use.

⬤ The potato plant stores starch in tubers on underground stems.

In Focus: Sugar

Sugar cane is a tropical grass with thick stems, called canes, that grow to about 6.5 ft. (2 m). Each year, the canes are harvested and crushed to extract a sugary juice. The juice is boiled to make a thick syrup and then cooled, so that sugar crystals form. This is raw sugar. Pieces of stem and other impurities are removed by further heating and washing.

◀ Sugar cane is grown as a crop, because its stem is rich in sugar. Machines cut the stems at ground level.

Plants and their environment

Plants grow in many different habitats around the world, from steamy tropical rain forests and hot deserts, to frozen mountain tops. Plants cannot move around, so they have to be able to cope with their environment. Plants that are adapted to their environment grow well, but those less suited to their surroundings do not survive.

Investigate: Plant adaptations

Look around your home, yard, or local park to see if you can find plants that are adapted to surviving in dry conditions. These types of plant may have thick, fleshy leaves to store water. The leaves may be covered by a shiny cuticle to reduce water loss. Some may have gray, hairy leaves that reflect the heat and reduce water loss.

○ This cactus has spines instead of leaves. The spines protect the plant from grazing animals.

Desert plants

A cactus is a plant that is adapted to life in deserts, where there is no rain for many months and high day-time temperatures. The leaves of cactus plants are reduced to spines to reduce the surface area from which water can evaporate. Their stems are covered by a thick, waxy cuticle, which reduces water loss even more. The stems can expand to take up lots of water when it rains. Many other desert plants have leaves that are thick and fleshy, and can store water, such as the stone plant, which has leaves that look like small pebbles.

Alpine plants

Plants that grow high on mountain slopes have to cope with an environment that is windy, bitterly cold, and covered with snow in the winter. Most alpine plants are low-growing plants that hug the ground. In this position, they can be sheltered from the wind. In the winter, the layer of snow protects them and insulates them from the freezing conditions.

Aquatic plants

Aquatic plants, such as seaweeds and water weeds, are plants that live in water. These plants need light, too, so they are found in shallow water or they float near the surface. They have air spaces in their stems and leaves to keep them buoyant. Some plants, such as bulrushes and yellow irises, prefer boggy ground, so they are found growing close to water or in shallow water where their leaves grow above the water.

⬤ This spider monkey uses its long legs and tail to move through the trees of the rain forest with ease.

In Focus: Trees for shelter

Plants provide animals with shelter as well as food. A large tree may be home to hundreds of different types of animal. Birds nest in trees, while snakes lie in wait among the branches watching for prey. Insects burrow under bark and into leaves to lay their eggs. The sloth, a type of mammal, lives its entire life hanging from branches. Other animals roost on trees at night, for example, bats and birds.

Seeds

The life cycle of a flowering plant starts with a seed. A seed contains an embryo, which can grow into a new plant. There is also a store of food, which the embryo needs to fuel its growth. This food store is usually fat and a carbohydrate, such as starch. Around the outside of the seed is a tough outer coat called the testa, which protects the embryo.

Large or small?

The size and number of seeds varies from plant to plant. In general, a plant that grows tiny seeds produces lots of them, but a plant that has large seeds produces a small number. For example, orchids have tiny seeds, each seed weighing just a tiny fraction of an ounce.

A single orchid plant may release many thousands of seeds. In comparison, a broad bean grows a seed that is up to an inch long.

The seed is packed with food, which is why people like to eat them! Each broad bean plant makes several hundred plump seeds. Even these relatively large seeds are small compared with the largest seed in the world. This is the huge seed of the coco-de-mer, a type of palm found only in the Seychelles. A single seed weighs as much as 44 pounds (20 kilograms).

◀ Each broad bean seed is swollen with starch and proteins. We need protein in our food for healthy growth.

Investigate: Seeds

Seeds are an important part of our diet. Look in a food cupboard at home and at the foods on sale in stores, and see if you can answer these questions. What types of seed are used in breakfast cereals? Which seeds can be used to make bread? Which are described as staple foods? Which are eaten as vegetables?

⬤ Lentils, kidney beans, and peas can be dried and stored for future use.

Lying in the soil

Soil is full of seeds, many of which can lie dormant for years, waiting for the right conditions to grow. Digging turns over the soil and brings seeds closer to the surface, where they can start to grow. Some weed seeds can survive in the ground for more than 100 years. Scientists have even managed to grow a plant from a seed thought to be about 1,300 years old.

In Focus: Oil-rich seeds

Some plants produce seeds that are rich in oil. Many of these plants are grown as crops, for example, oil palm, olive, sunflower, oilseed rape, and soybean. The seeds are collected and pressed to extract the oil. The oil is put to many uses. For example, it can be used to make cooking oil and margarine, or as a fuel in engines. Fuels made from plant oils are usually sold as biodiesel. Oil from seeds can also be burned to provide heat and hot water for homes.

◀ The seeds of the oilseed rape plant are small, but they are filled with an oil that can be extracted and put to many uses, such as in cooking and as animal feed.

New life

The first stage of the plant's life cycle is when the seed bursts into life. This is called germination. The new seedling pushes above the soil and new leaves appear. The plant grows larger until it flowers.

Germination

All seeds need water and oxygen to germinate. Many seeds also need the right temperature, for example, seeds from tropical regions may not germinate unless the temperature is 68°F (20°C) or more. Many tree seeds from temperate parts of the world, such as Europe and North America, need to experience several weeks of very cold temperatures before they germinate. This makes sure that they do not germinate after a short warm spell in winter. Some seeds, such as lettuce seeds, will not germinate unless there is some light, so they must be scattered on the surface of the soil and not buried.

⬤ Banksia plants like these are found in Australia. They produce large seed cases that stay on the plant until a fire passes through the woodland. The case is burned, releasing the seeds onto the ground where they germinate.

In Focus: Fire and germination

In some habitats, fires are common, for example, grassland and woodlands in parts of Australia. The trees have a thick bark for protection against fire, so they are not harmed if a fire sweeps through. The seeds of some trees and shrubs only germinate after a fire. The trigger to germinate is smoke. By germinating after a fire, the seeds can germinate in bare ground covered in ash that is rich in nutrients.

First growth

When all the conditions are right, the seed will germinate. First, the seed takes up water. This causes the seed to swell and the testa splits open. Seeds need energy to grow and this comes from their food store. Water entering the seed is the trigger for the food to be used. The first sign of germination is the appearance of the shoot. Then the first root, or radicle, appears. The shoot always grows upward, pushing out of the soil as the roots grow down into the ground. Soon after the shoot appears, the first leaves open. The first leaves of some seedlings are small, round, and fat. They are called cotyledons and they are full of food.

⚫ When a broad bean seed germinates, the shoot appears first, followed by the radicle. The shoot extends upward while the radicle grows down.

Investigate: Nutrients

You can find out how important nutrients are to a plant by performing a simple experiment. Take some broad bean seeds, paper towel, and two jelly jars. Roll up some paper towel and place it in each jar. Push the seeds down between the glass and paper. Add some water to the jar, but make sure the seeds are out of the water. Once the seeds have germinated, add a few drops of liquid plant fertilizer to the water of one jar. Do not add anything to the other jar. After a few weeks, you should see that the seedlings with the nutrients grow better than those without.

Plant nutrients

Plants need a constant supply of nutrients for healthy growth. The most important nutrients are nitrates, phosphates, and potassium, all of which are found dissolved in soil water. Without the right quantity of nutrients, a plant will not grow properly. One common symptom of a plant not getting enough nutrients is the yellowing of its leaves.

Flowers

Many plants produce bright-colored, eye-catching flowers. People find them attractive and grow them in yards, gardens, and parks. Flowers are also attractive to insects and other animals. These creatures help flowers to play an essential role in the life cycle of a plant.

Flower parts

A typical flower is made up of a number of parts, each of which has a specific role. The two parts involved directly with reproduction are the stamen and carpel. The stamen is the male part and it consists of an anther, which produces pollen, and a stalk called a filament. Pollen is the mass of tiny, yellow dustlike particles released from the anthers. Inside each particle of pollen is a male cell. The female part is called the carpel, and it consists of a stigma, joined to the ovary by the style. Inside the ovary is an ovule that contains the egg.

A flower bud is usually protected by a number of green leaflike sepals. When the flower opens, the sepals drop off or are pushed down. The petals unfurl to form a ring around the stamens and carpels. Some flowers have nectaries at the base of their petals. Nectaries make nectar, a sugary liquid that attracts insects and birds.

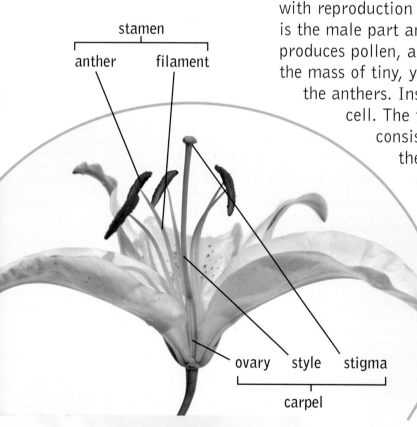

stamen
anther   filament

ovary   style   stigma
carpel

⬤ The lily flower has several anthers that form a ring around the central carpel.

In Focus: Garden flowers

The bright-colored flowers that we see in yards and gardens have been bred from wild flowers. For example, the garden rose has been bred from the wild dog rose. Plant breeders have selected plants with the best flowers and used them to produce new plants. Today, the garden rose has large flowers with many petals, and a lovely perfume. The wild dog rose has a much smaller flower with just five petals.

Simple and complex flowers

Flowers vary greatly in shape and number of flower parts. Some flowers are very simple, for example, a buttercup has five petals and five sepals. More complex flowers have petals that are joined together. For example, the honeysuckle has petals that are joined to form a tube. The daisy looks as if it is one flower, but it is really made up of many small flowers joined together. Some flowers do not have any petals at all. The red flower of the poinsettia, a popular Christmas plant, is really leaves.

⬤ The petals of the meadow clary flower are joined together to form a tube. The bottom petal is large and forms a landing platform for insects.

Investigate: Flower structure

One way to identify a plant is to look closely at its flower structure. Scientists count the number of petals, and look to see if the petals are separate or joined together. They also count the other parts of the flower, such as the sepals, stamens, and stigmas. See if you can identify some common wild flowers. You will need a magnifying glass and a guide book on wild flowers. Start with some flowers that you can identify already, then move on to some you do not know.

Plant reproduction

The most important stage in the plant life cycle is reproduction. This is when the male cell joins with the egg cell to form an embryo, which grows into a new plant. There are two parts to plant reproduction—pollination and fertilization.

Insect pollinators

Pollination is the transfer of pollen from the anthers to the stigma. Pollen can be transferred in different ways. The most common is when animals, such as insects, birds, and bats, visit flowers and are covered in pollen. Insect-pollinated flowers attract their pollinators by having bright-colored petals or strong scents that are easy for insects to detect. They also produce nectar, a food for insects. Insects pick up the pollen as they crawl over the flower.

In some tube-shaped flowers, when an insect such as a bee lands at the entrance, the weight of the animal causes the anthers to drop down and leave pollen on its back.

◔ A bee stores pollen in the special pollen basket on its back leg, so it can carry the pollen back to the hive.

In Focus: Plants and pollinators

Most flowers are pollinated by a variety of animals, but a few flowers have just one specific pollinator. For example, many orchids growing in the rain forest rely on one type of bee to pollinate their flowers. Without this pollinator, they would not survive. If anything happened to the pollinator, for example, if it died due to habitat loss or climate change, then the plant would die out too.

Wind pollinators

A few plants rely on the wind or water to carry their pollen away. A wind pollinated plant has separate male and female flowers. The male flower consists of lots of small flowers on a stalk which form a catkin. This dangles in the wind, shedding pollen that is then carried to the female flower, a small structure made up of large, feathery stigmas.

Pollinating other flowers

Self-pollination is when a flower pollinates itself. Although seeds can still be produced, the new plants may not be as healthy or as large as the parent plant. Cross-pollination occurs when pollen from one plant pollinates a flower of a different plant. Many flowers have both male and female parts, so they have ways of making sure they do not pollinate their own flowers. For example, they may release their pollen before the carpel is formed. Some plants have flowers that have just male or female parts, but others may have separate male and female plants.

⬥ Clouds of pollen are released when wind moves these catkins.

Investigate: Flowers

Some common plants make flowers of one sex, for example, zucchini. If you look inside the flower of a zucchini, you will find either stamens or stigmas, but never both. The fruits only form on the female flowers.

Fruits and seeds

After pollination has occurred, the male cell in the pollen must fertilize the female egg so the seeds can be produced. Once the pollen has landed on the stigma, the pollen grows a long tube that extends down through the style to the ovary and ovule. The male cell moves along the tube into the ovary and joins with the female egg inside the ovule. This is fertilization. The new cell is called an embryo.

Investigate: Pollen

Using a small paint brush, remove some pollen from the anthers of a flower. Use a magnifying glass to look at it. Can you see much? Now dissolve some sugar in a little water. Place a drop of the sugary water on a dark surface and gently drop some pollen on the water. The pollen will start growing and after about 30 minutes, you should be able to see long tubes extending from the pollen grains.

After fertilization

Once fertilization has happened, changes take place in the flower. The petals and sepals wither and drop off. The ovary starts to swell up and becomes the fruit. The ovule becomes the seed. The ovary protects and nourishes the seeds as they develop.

Fruit types

There are two main types of fruit—dry fruits and fleshy fruits. Examples of dry fruits include the bean and the sycamore. The ovary of the bean plant grows into a pod. Each pod contains a number of seeds. As the pod ripens, it gets drier, until it eventually splits apart and flings out the seeds. The fruit of a sycamore tree grows a wing that helps to disperse the seed. Nuts, such as the acorn of the oak tree, are dry fruits, too. The wall of the ovary swells up and becomes hard to protect the large seed inside.

Other fruits, such as peaches and plums, are fleshy. As the fruit ripens, the flesh becomes soft. Often the flesh is sweet tasting. The thick flesh covers a hard stone, which surrounds the seed. Tomatoes and sweet peppers have a fleshy fruit containing many seeds.

The seeds of a pear (on the left) are surrounded by the fruit's sweet-tasting flesh. The seed pod that is the fruit of the stinking iris (on the right) dries out and releases the seeds.

In Focus: Super fruits

Many fruits, such as cranberries, red grapes, and pomegranates, are described as "super foods," because they are particularly good for people's health. One of the latest juices to appear in the stores is made from the açai berry, which grows on a palm tree in the Amazon rain forest. All these fruits have been found to contain large amounts of substances called antioxidants. These are thought to have several medical benefits, such as helping the body to fight infection, aiding blood circulation, and preventing heart disease. There are claims they may even help against some types of cancer.

Orchards of orange trees are found in the warmer parts of the world, such as Southern Spain, California, and Florida.

Spreading seeds

Another critical stage in a plant's life cycle is the scattering of its seeds. It is important that the seeds are dispersed away from the parent plant. If the seeds drop too close to the parent plant, when they grow, they will compete with the parent plant for water and nutrients.

Eaten by animals

Seeds are dispersed in different ways. Seeds from fleshy fruits are usually carried by animals, which eat these fruits then spit out the seed far away from the plant. Squirrels help to disperse tree fruits. They collect fruits such as acorns and bury them in the ground to eat in the winter. Sometimes, fruits are carried away by animals on their fur, for example, the burdock, which has hooked spikes that grip the animal's coat.

In Focus: Birds and mistletoe

The mistletoe is a parasitic plant that is found on trees such as apple trees. It uses birds to disperse its fruits. The fruits of the mistletoe are very sticky and they stick to a bird's beak. The bird removes the fruit by rubbing its beak against the bark of a tree. The fruit is left stuck to the bark, the perfect place for the seed, because it germinates and grows into the tree.

⬆ This hyacinth macaw is eating the fruits of a palm tree.

The seeds of some plants will not germinate unless they have passed through the gut of an animal. The testa is weakened as the seed passes along the gut. The seeds pass out in the animal's droppings and fall to the ground. This creates perfect conditions for germination. The seed is protected by the dung and the dung is full of nutrients.

Wind and water

Seeds can also be dispersed by wind and water. Dandelion fruits have a feathery "parachute" that catches the wind. Sycamore and maple fruits have a wing so they glide to the ground. Water disperses the seeds of aquatic plants and even the large fruits of the coconut palm.

⬤ Each dandelion seed has a feathery parachute that catches the wind so it is carried away.

⬤ Coconuts float, so they are carried away by currents in the ocean and are eventually washed up on a beach, where they germinate.

Investigate: Seedlings

Find out how far seeds have spread by looking for seedlings. Find a large tree, such as an oak, birch, or sycamore, growing on its own in a field or park. Look around the tree for its seedlings. Make a small map showing the tree and the position of all the seedlings around the tree. Sometimes, you may find more in one particular area in relation to the parent tree. This is because the wind blows mainly from one direction.

Runners, stolons, and bulbs

Most flowering plants reproduce by producing seeds. However, some plants can reproduce without seeds. They use a method called asexual reproduction. This involves a single plant producing identical copies of itself.

In Focus: Identical plants

Many of the thousands of bedding plants that are on sale in garden centers and plant nurseries have been produced from cuttings. Growers select parent plants with the desired features, such as flower color or scent, then take lots of cuttings. This way, the growers know that the new plants will be identical to the parent plants. If they grew plants from seeds, there is the chance that the new plants would be different from the parent.

◀ The Mexican hat plant is unusual because it grows miniature plantlets along the edge of its leaves. When they are large enough, they drop to the ground and grow into new plants.

New plants

A strawberry plant is a good example of a plant that reproduces asexually. In the summer, a parent strawberry plant produces a special stem called a runner that grows along the ground. A new plant grows at the tip. Sometimes, several plants form along a runner. This form of reproduction happens very fast, so one strawberry plant can become several in a short period of time. Many grasses reproduce in a similar way, by producing runners under the ground. When you pull up the parent plant, you see a white runner that grows through the soil. Raspberry plants multiply by growing an underground stem called a stolon. Plants such as ash, elm, and rose produce suckers, which appear above ground close to the parent plant.

This strawberry plant has produced several runners. A new plant forms at the tip of the runner.

runner

Bulbs

Many plants produce bulbs, for example, daffodils, tulips, and onions. A bulb is a swelling at the base of a stem. During the summer, the plant photosynthesizes and builds up a store of food in the bulb. In the fall, the shoot dies back and the plant survives the winter underground. In springtime, the plant uses the food in the bulb to produce new growth. Each year, tiny bulbils form beside the main bulb and each grows up into a new plant.

Investigate: Taking cuttings

Many gardeners make new plants by taking a cutting from a plant. The cuttings grow into plants that are identical to the parent plant. You can try this yourself by taking cuttings of a plant such as a geranium. Cut off a short piece of stem and remove the lower leaves. Place the cutting in a small container of water and place on a window ledge. After a couple of weeks or so, you will see tiny white roots growing from the base of the cutting. Once you have some roots, you can plant the rooted cutting in a pot of compost.

Rotting plants

The final part of a plant's life cycle is when the plant dies. The plant decays or breaks down, and nutrients are released into the ground to be used by other plants.

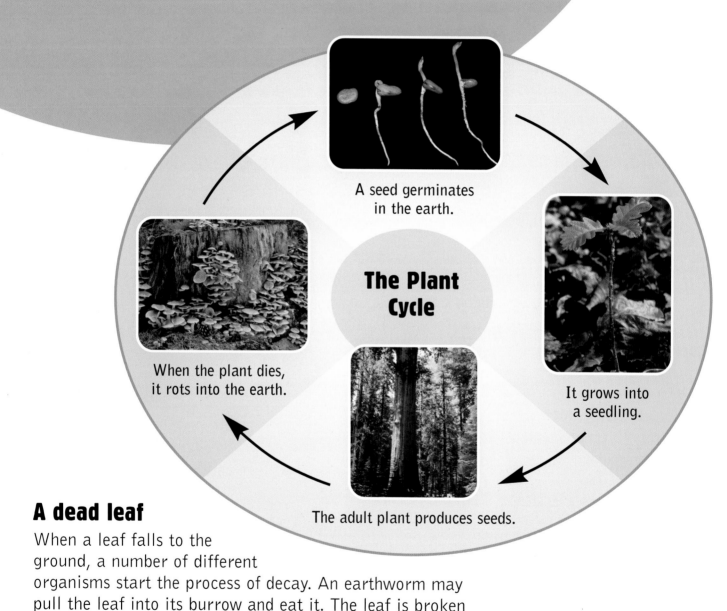

A seed germinates in the earth.

The Plant Cycle

When the plant dies, it rots into the earth.

It grows into a seedling.

The adult plant produces seeds.

A dead leaf

When a leaf falls to the ground, a number of different organisms start the process of decay. An earthworm may pull the leaf into its burrow and eat it. The leaf is broken down into smaller pieces as it passes through the earthworm's gut. The remains pass out of the earthworm and onto the surface of the soil as a worm cast.

Wood lice feed on dead leaves, too. The most important decomposers are microorganisms, such as bacteria and fungi. The role of decomposers is to complete the breakdown of the leaf and return all the nutrients that were locked up in the leaf, back to the soil.

In Focus: The world's oldest living plants

Some plants only live for a few weeks, but others live for thousands of years. Some of the world's oldest living plants include a King's holly growing in the Tasmanian rain forest in Australia, which is thought to be 43,000 years old, an Australian eucalyptus tree that may be 12,000 years old, and a creosote bush growing in the Mojave Desert in California that is estimated to be 11,700 years old.

⬤ Lots of fungi live in leaf litter. In the fall, colorful toadstools, such as this fly agaric, appear above ground.

Leaf litter

The layer of dead leaves on a woodland floor is an important wildlife habitat. There are animals such as slugs, snails, springtails, millipedes, and worms, all feeding on the dead leaves. They are eaten by predators such as spiders and centipedes. A whole food web can be found within a small area of woodland leaf litter.

Investigate: Rotting leaves

You can see how quickly leaves decay in this simple investigation, which can be carried out in the summer. Take ten leaves from each of three different kinds of tree. Place each set of leaves in a plastic food net (such as those in which oranges are sold). Now bury the nets in the ground, just below the surface. Mark the spot so you can find it again, and leave for a month. Then dig the nets up and examine all the leaves. Have they started to decay? Put the nets back and leave them for another month before digging them up again. Which type of leaf is the most decayed?

Plants and global warming

Global warming is a big threat to the world's plants. It is caused by gases known as greenhouses gases, such as carbon dioxide and methane, in the Earth's atmosphere.

Greenhouse gases

Greenhouse gases trap heat in the atmosphere. Their job is to keep the Earth at the right temperature for life to survive. However, more greenhouse gases are being produced by the activities of people, when they burn fuels, such as coal, gas, and oil, in power stations and as fuel for vehicles. As more greenhouse gases are released into the atmosphere, more heat than is necessary is being trapped. This is causing the Earth's surface to get gradually warmer.

⬥ In the United Kingdom, spring is getting earlier. Bluebells usually flower in April and May, but in recent years, the flowers have been appearing in March.

Investigate: Early spring

Keep a diary and record the weather and the date when you first see a particular type of spring flower, for example, the first daffodil, English bluebell, or foxglove. Now use the Internet or visit a local history center to see if you can find historical records that show flowering times in your area. See if the dates on which you saw the flowers are earlier or later than those shown in the records.

Climate change

The temperature may only increase by a few degrees, but this is enough to disrupt climates. It is likely that it will get warmer farther north, with the result, for example, that southern Britain may have a climate more like that of southern France today. Also, there may be summer droughts, or more extreme weather, such as strong winds, severe storms, and flooding.

⬆ Drought in this part of Australia has caused the cattle to overgraze the grassland, so now the soil is bare.

These changes will alter habitats. Animals may be able to move away, but plants cannot. If the climate changes, plants will either have to adapt or die. If animals move away, plants may lose their pollinators. Spring may come early and the flowers appear before the pollinators. This disrupts the plant cycle and means the plants cannot make seeds. New animals may move into a habitat and start grazing on plants, and this could also threaten the plant cycle.

In Focus: Why are rain forests important?

Rain forests are home to more species of animals and plants than any other habitat. Unfortunately, the forests are being cleared for their wood and to make space for farming and other uses. All plants take up carbon dioxide, so removing the forests adds carbon dioxide to the atmosphere. Some scientists think as much as one-third of the carbon dioxide produced in the world each year comes from rain forest clearance. Protecting these forests will not only save the animals and plants, but help to stop global warming, too.

29

Glossary

adapted Suited.

anther The male part of a flower that produces the pollen.

antioxidants Substances that help the body repair damaged cells.

aquatic Living in water.

biodiesel Fuel for diesel engines that is made from plant oils.

biomass The living mass of an organism.

carbon dioxide A gas found in the atmosphere. We breathe in oxygen and breathe out carbon dioxide.

carnivore An animal that eats meat.

carpel The female part of a flower, consisting of a stigma, style, and ovary.

catkin A tangling chain of male flowers that produces lots of pollen.

cell The smallest unit of a living organism. Plants are made up of millions of cells.

cellulose A substance made from sugar, found in the cell wall of all plant cells.

chlorophyll The green pigment in plants.

chloroplasts Small structures found in some plant cells, chloroplasts are filled with chlorophyll.

cotyledon A seed leaf, the first leaf produced by a seedling.

cuticle A waxy covering on a leaf.

cytoplasm The jelly-like material that fills a cell.

decay To break down.

deciduous Having leaves that drop off at the end of the growing season.

decomposer An organism that brings about decay.

embryo The earliest stage in the life of a plant or animal.

evergreen A plant that has leaves all year round.

fertilize When a male cell (or sperm) fuses with a female cell (egg) to form an embryo.

filament The stalk of the stamen, it joins the anther to the flower.

fruit A seed case, formed from the ovary.

germinate To begin to grow.

greenhouse gases Gases, such as carbon dioxide and methane, that trap heat in the atmosphere.

herbivore An animal that eats plants.

hypha (pl. hyphae) The threadlike structure that makes up the body of many fungi.

membrane The very thin, sheetlike structure that forms a barrier around a cell.

nectary The nectar-producing part of a flower.

nutrient A substance needed for healthy growth.

ovary The female part of a flower that contains the ovule. The ovary develops into a fruit.

ovule The female part of the flower that contains the egg. The ovule develops into a seed.

parasite An organism that lives in or on another organism and causes harm to that organism.

petiole The stalk of a leaf.

photosynthesis The process by which a plant makes sugar and oxygen from carbon dioxide and water in the presence of light.

pollen A dustlike particle that contains a male cell.

pollinate To transfer pollen from the anther to the stigma.

pollinator An animal, such as an insect, bird, or bat, that carries pollen from the anther to the stigma.

radicle The first root of a seedling.

root hair A tiny extension from a cell in the root, important in the uptake of nutrients and water from the soil.

runner A stem that grows over the surface of the soil and grows new plants at its tip.

seed A structure produced by a plant that can grow into a new plant.

stamen The male part of a flower consisting of an anther and filament.

starch A carbohydrate made by plants.

stigma The sticky part of the female carpel at the top of the style.

stolon A stem that grows over the surface of the soil and grows new plants at its tip; also called a runner.

stomata Tiny pores in a leaf that allow gases to enter or leave a plant.

style The part of the carpel that joins the stigma to the ovary.

sugar A sweet-tasting carbohydrate.

testa The outer covering of a seed.

Further Information

Books

How We Use Plants For Food
by Sally Morgan
(PowerKids Press, 2008)

The Life Cycle of a Flower
by Molly Aloian
(Crabtree Publishing Company, 2004)

Web Sites

Due to the changing nature of Internet links, PowerKids Press has developed an online list of Web sites related to the subject of this book. This site is updated regularly. Please use this link to access this list: www.powerkidslinks.com/natc/plant

Index

Numbers in **bold** refer to pictures.

anther 16, **16**, 30, 31
antioxidants 21, 30
aquatic plants 11, 23

biomass 4, 30
bulbs 24, 25

carbon dioxide 4, 28, 29, 30, 31
carnivores 4
carpel 16, **16**, 17, 30, 31
cells 6, **6**
cellulose 6, 30
chlorophyll 6, 8, 30
chloroplasts 6, 8, 30
cone-bearing plants 5
cotyledons 15
cytoplasm 6, 30

decay 27, 30
deciduous 7, 30
decomposers 27, **27**
diet 5, 13
drought 7, 10, 29, **29**

energy 4, 8, 15
evergreen 7, 30

ferns 5, 29

fertilization 18, 20
filament 16, **16**, 30, 31
flowering plants 5, **17**, **18**, **19**, **21**, **23**, 24, **25**, **28**
fruits 20, 21, **21**, **22**, 23, **23**
fuel 12, 13, 28, 30
fungi 27, **27**, 30

germination 14, 15, **15**, 23
global warming 28, 29
greenhouse gases 28, 30

habitats 10, 14, 29
herbivores 4, 5, **5**

insects 11, 16, 18, **18**

leaves 4, 5, 6, 7, **7**, **8**, 9, 10, 11, 14, 15, 17, 24, 25, 27, 30
liverworts 5

mosses 5

nectar 16, 18, 30
nectaries 16
nucleus 6
nutrients 7, 14, 15, 22, 23, 26, 27, 31

omnivores 4
ovary 16, **16**, 20, 21, 30, 31
ovule 16, 20, 31
oxygen 9, 14, 30, 31

parasites 7, **7**

photosynthesis 4, 6, 7, 8, 31,
plant cycle 5, 22, 26, **26**, 29
pollen 16, 17, 18, **18**, 19, **19**, 20, 30, 31
pollination 18, 19, 20
producers 4

reproduction 3, 7, 16, 18, 24, 25
roots 5, 6, 7, 9, 15, 25
runners 24, 25, **25**

seed dispersal 20, 21, **22**, **23**
seeds 5, 12, **12**, 13, **13**, 14, 15, 19, 20, 21, **21**, 22, 23, **23**, 24, 29
sepal 16, 17, 20
stamen 16, 30, 31
starches 4, 32
stems 3, 4, 6, 7, 9, 10, 11, 32
stigma 16, 18, 20, 30, 31, 32
stolons 24
stomata 31
style 16, **16**, 19, 20, 30, 31
sugars 4

testa 12, 15, 23, 31

vacuole 6

water 4, 7, 9, 10, 11, 13, 14, 15, 19, 20, 22, 23, 25, 30, 31